Fighting T[...]

Photo by Sally Cookson

Paul Cookson was born in 1961, brought up near Preston, and now lives in Retford, Notts. He has worked as a poet since 1989, performing in schools and libraries, and at literature festivals and events across the world. As well as being Poet-in-Residence for The National Football Museum and Everton in the Community, he is Writer-in-Residence for Sing Together, which involves 125 Lancastrian schools and over 5000 children and 400 teachers. He is also Poet Laureate for Slade, has written a book of poems about the band and performed with Noddy Holder, Jim Lea and Don Powell. He is now part of Don Powell's Occasional Flames and is currently working on their second album. Paul has more than sixty titles to his name and over a million book sales, and with a quarter of a million copies sold, the anthology *The Works* has become a teacher's 'poetry Bible'. You can visit his website at www.paulcooksonpoet.co.uk and follow all of his poems daily on Twitter @paulcooksonpoet.

Selected works

For adults:
Touched by The Band of Nod – The Slade Poems •
The Saturday Men •

For children:
Football 4 Every 1 ★
The Very Best of Paul Cookson ★
Paul Cookson's Joke Shop ★
There's a Crocodile in the House ♦

As Editor:
The Works ★
100 Brilliant Poems for Children ★
Fire Burn, Cauldron Bubble ▲

• Published by A Twist in the Tale & available at paulcooksonpoet.co.uk
★ Published by Pan Macmillan ♦ Published by Otter Barry Books
▲ Published by Bloomsbury

FIGHTING TALK
PAUL COOKSON

A COVID-19 POETRY DIARY

Illustrated by Chris Riddell OBE

Very best wishes
Paul Cookson

Flapjack Press
www.flapjackpress.co.uk

Exploring the synergy between performance and the page

Published in 2020 by Flapjack Press
Salford, Gtr Manchester
⊕ flapjackpress.co.uk
f Flapjack Press 🐦 FlapjackPress

ISBN 978-1-8381185-0-1

All rights reserved
Copyright © Paul Cookson, 2020
⊕ paulcooksonpoet.co.uk
🐦 paulcooksonpoet 📷 paulcooksonpoet

Illustrated by Chris Riddell OBE
⊕ chrisriddellblog.tumblr.com
🐦 chrisriddell50 📷 chris_riddell

Cover by Martin Chatterton
⊕ worldofchatterton.com
🐦 MEChatterton 📷 edchatt

Printed by Imprint Digital
Upton Pyne, Exeter, Devon
⊕ digital.imprint.co.uk

This book is sold subject to the condition that is shall not by way of trade or otherwise be lent, re-sold, hired out or otherwise circulated in any form, binding or cover other than that in which it is published and without a similar condition including this condition being imposed on the subsequent purchaser.

FSC MANCHESTER
City of Literature

I'd like to dedicate this book to Joan Burton – always Mrs Burton though. She was my primary school teacher (Little Hoole Country Primary School, if you must know) and has commented on almost a daily basis. Plus, she's given me the best marks ever. Thanks Miss.

Thanks to all of you on social media who have regularly commented on, shared, encouraged, retweeted and liked these poems. You have been the inspiration to carry on.

Also, big thanks to Martin and Chris – great to have two friends and brilliant illustrators on board.

Contents

Introduction		*10*
#1	The Day the World Stood Still	15
#2	But I'm Not	16
#3	What to Do With All This Time?	17
#4	Connection	18
#5	Now is the Time	19
#6	Like Any Other Day	20
#7	And on the Seventh Day …	21
#8	This is the New Normal	22
#9	Oh … the Irony	24
#10	Haiku	25
#11	April the Second	25
#12	Still	26
#13	The Worst	27
#14	Sunshine and a Sunny Day	28
#15	Viral	29
#16	A Cup of Tea and a Good Night's Sleep	30
#17	I Will Not Clap for Boris	30
#18	I Was Late to the Party – But You'd Already Left	31
#19	Not Walking Alone	32
#20	Silver Linings	33
#21	Easter Sunday: One	33
#22	Easter Sunday: Two – Haiku	34
#23	An Oldie but a Goodie	35
#24	Named	36
#25	Covidiot	37
#26	Bad Rock Puns Warning …	38
#27	Can You Hear Us Major Tom?	39
#28	Norman	40
#29	Cornflakes	41
#30	Leaders Failing to Lead Us	43

#31	Not a Good Time for My Business	44
#32	Nobody Famous Died Today	45
#33	I Seem to Be Agreeing with Somebody Called Piers	46
#34	Thank Our Lucky Stars	48
#35	Saturday Night Lockdown Blockbusters	50
#36	Priti Obvious, Priti Vacant	50
#37	Overheard in a Supermarket Queue …	51
#38	COVID-19 Killed the Radio Star …	51
#39	On the Passing of Grandparents …	52
#40	The Only Thing That's Doctored …	53
#41	At Least the Rain Will Keep the Idiots In	55
#42	The Satanic Versus …	56
#43	Solace	58
#44	Hand in Hand	59
#45	Punk Rock Moustache	60
#46	Here to Stay Each Day	61
#47	Fighting Talk	62
#48	These Could Be the Good Old Days	63
#49	V.E. Day Celebrations	64
#50	Another Day, Another Headline, Another Poem	65
#51	Haiku for Little Richard	66
#52	A Mess of Contradictions	66
#53	Stay Alert Boris	67
#54	Over to You	69
#55	Schools Can't Cope with an Outbreak of Nits …	70
#56	You Cannot Social Distance in a School	71
#57	Let Our Teachers Be Heroes	73
#58	Education – Education – Differentiation	74
#59	Mr Hancock's Half Hour	74
#60	Blackbird on a Sunday Morning	75
#61	We're All in This Together	76
#62	Are You Sitting Comfortably? …	77
#63	He Was	79
#64	Aftermath	80

#65	Missed	82
#66	Too	84
#67	Comings and Goings	85
#68	Not So Very Long Ago	86
#69	Meanwhile, in Other News …	87
#70	This Poem is True	89
#71	No Regrets	91
#72	I Think That I'm in Love with Emily Maitlis	93
#73	Impartiality	94
#74	Civic Duty	95
#75	A Happy Song for Us to Sing to Celebrate …	96
#76	Down by the Riverbank	98
#77	Prayer for the First Day of School	99
#78	When the First Child Dies in School	100
#79	The Truth That's in The Bible is Lost …	101
#80	Take the Knee	103
#81	The President and The Bible	104
#82	Hell Raiser	105
#83	Too Much to Ask?	106
#84	Phone Call From a Friend	107
#85	Malady in the U.K.	109
#86	Weekend Haiku Thoughts	110
#87	Are We Being Served?	110
#88	Empathy Day or … Irony Day?	111
#89	Lesson – the Danger … or is it Lessen the Danger?	111
#90	I'm Forever Bursting …	111
#91	Sometimes	112
#92	The Singer Sings His Song – with a Poet's Heart	113
#93	Welcome Back	114
#94	Truth	115
#95	Saint Patrick's Day	117
#96	I'm Not Looking Forward to Football Again	118
#97	In a League of His Own	119
#98	Problem or Solution	120

#99	Songbird	122
#100	Tired	123
#101	All the World is a Plague – a Sonnet	124
#102	Boris – On It? Boris – Sonnet	126
#103	Today's News – in Limerick Form	126
#104	Ignorance is Bliss	127
#105	No More Daily Briefings	129
#106	Back to Life – Back to Reality?	130
#107	Churchill Would Be Proud	131
#108	Hindsight	132
#109	He Wants His Churchill Moment	134
#110	Fit as a Butcher's Dog	136
#111	So Many Reasons, Mister Rosen	139
#112	Boz the Builder	141
#113	Let Me Tell You How I Count the Days	142
#114	Can't Wait for Saturday Night	144

Introduction

Hello friends.

You have leant me your ears.

I never set out to write a poem a day. It just sort of happened when Lockdown happened.

Like many, I suddenly had more time and I noticed that Chris Riddell was producing a cartoon a day and sharing them. I thought I'd try that with poetry – set myself a task of writing something new every day and then share it on Facebook, Twitter and Instagram.

At that stage, I had no idea how long I would do this for – or indeed, whether I'd find something to write about every day. Yet here we are. Here they are – in this book.

They were instant responses to whatever was happening on that day – whether personal or in the wider world. As such, constant themes and phrases, clichés even, appear on a regular basis. I've tried to resist the urge to edit, but some have changed a little in layout, chronology and not every single poem written has made it here as some were similar or repetitive.

The inspiration hasn't just been what has been happening, but the reactions I've had. There have been a regular group who have commented, shared, liked and encouraged throughout. To all of you – you know who are – thank you so much.

Thanks to Paul Neads at Flapjack for the quickest response to a book ever! I emailed one morning and he replied in the afternoon.

Also, Martin Chatterton (long-time collaborator, friend and fellow Evertonian) for his wonderful work on the cover.

Great to have Chris Riddell on board too – it all started with his pictures, so it's brilliant that he was able to contribute.

We all thought it might be over by now and back to normal – whatever that may be. It isn't and we're not. I've no idea when my school visits and gigs will start again. In the meantime, I'll carry on writing a poem a day ... ready for Volume Two. If you want a sneak preview of the cover, turn to the back page now. You did, didn't you? Good, isn't it?

Stay safe.

Paul Cookson
August 2020

Fighting Talk

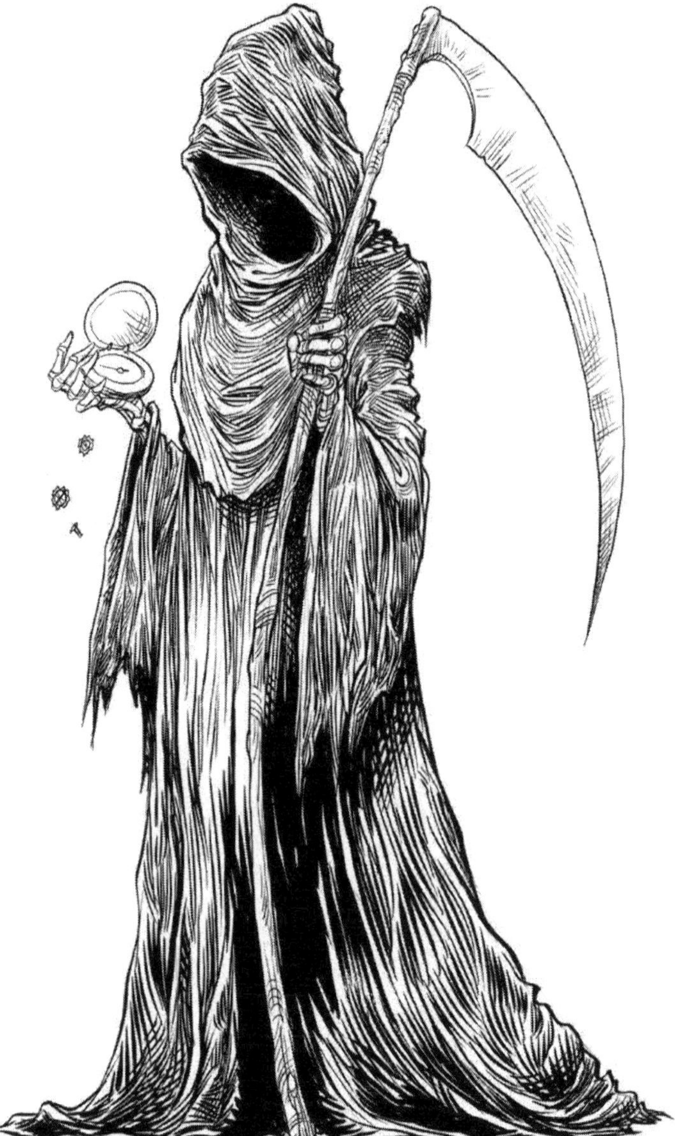
CHRIS RIDDELL

The Day the World Stood Still

#1 / 23:03:2020

More than just – trouble at t'mill
More than flu to make you ill
More than a virus – it will kill
The day the world stood still

No quick fix, no magic pill
Vaccination numbers – nil
Feel the fear, fear the chill
The day the world stood still

Now we've too much time to fill
Going to be a long, long time until
We do those things we know we will
The day the world stood still

This is the day
This is the day
This the day world stood

But I'm Not

#2 / 24:03:2020

Today, I should have been
At a school in Stoke-on-Trent
But I'm not

Right now, I should be mid-performance
Laughter and audience participation echoing
Like pantomime – but with better rhymes
But I'm not

I'm here, home
With a cup of tea and biscuits
A brand new notebook and pen
And this poem
Which I wouldn't usually be writing

Small part of me – glad of the time here
Not too busy to take a breath
Have another cup of tea
And another biscuit – of course
But the rest of me
Worried

Really worried
Anxious about the crossings out
The cancellations in my diary
The immediate disappearance of work
And the uncertainty

What to Do With All This Time?

#3 / 25:03:2020

I suppose that I've always wanted
Much more time to write
But now that it's real and here
It doesn't feel quite right

> *And that can't be a rhyme*
> *Just because it's spelt differently*
> *It still sounds like the same word*
> *So I've failed already ...*

I could finish the novel I long-ago started
Complaining I never had the time
Go through all my files and notebooks
Unfinished poems, forgotten good lines

Sort out all the ideas and plans
The seeds that have fallen along the way
I bought a brand new notebook so maybe
I could even write a new poem every day ...

Connection
#4/ 26:03:2020

Doors open – we pause
And then – applause

That ripple effect
As isolates connect

A standing ovation
Appreciation

This strange communion
Our separate union

A simple act of hope
Together we vote

N.H.S.
Quite simply – yes

Now is the Time

#5 / 27:03:2020

Now is not the time to be cynical
More a time to be ecumenical

It isn't right, the centre or the left
It's trying to work out just what is the best

A crisis that is bringing us together
A virus that is changing us forever

But in this crisis let us recall
Those who did not value this at all

Those who thought that value was financial
Highest bidders, markets and potential

Private money-makers from elsewhere
Profit before people, cash before healthcare

If and when – eventually – those of us get through
Let us learn right now a value that is true

Cherish and protect at any cost
This jewel in our crown must not be lost

Safeguard doctors, nurses, safeguard health
For future generations – that's true wealth

Like Any Other Day

#6 / 28:03:2020

It could be like any other day
The house is quiet
The first cup of tea tastes good
And the birds outside still sing of heaven

It could be like any other day
I'm thinking of toast
Butter, marmalade – hey, even both
I can hear a clock ticking – or is it the fridge?

It could be like any other day
The T.V. is quiet
News is not news yet
Reality still slumbers, daydreaming

The sun still shines
Majestic as it ever did
Just like any other day
But it isn't

Heartache, worry, anxiety
Will soon overwhelm us
But for now, the house is quiet
And it could be like any other day

And on the Seventh Day …
#7 / 29:03:2020

Sunday used to be
    A day of rest

Now it's just another day
    Like all the rest

Sunday used to be
    The only day we'd pray

Now some of us are praying
    Every single day

This is the New Normal
#8 / 30:03:2020

This is the new normal
But if it isn't
More time to read and talk
Watch and listen
Socialise online
Isolate together in small groups and spaces
In this new normal
That is anything
But

This is the new normal
Baked potatoes
Toilet roll rationing
Hand gel wars
Empty streets and park
Closed pub doors
In this new normal
That is anything
But

This is the new normal
Experimental baking
Online front room fitness routines
Cleaning out the garden shed
And writing poems like this
In this new normal
That is anything
But

This is the new normal
But it isn't
The same arguments fester
The same disagreements jar
The petty and the life changing
Or the "just getting on each other's nerves"

All confined
All magnified
In this new normal
That is anything
But

Oh ... the Irony
#9 / 31:03:2020

Ironically
With more time on my hands
I've elected not to shave
And therefore grow a beard
For the duration
Thus giving me extra time
To write poems like this

> Pardon?
> What's that you say?
>
> *Start shaving again ...*

Haiku
#10 / 01:04:2020

The first of April
The fool still rules and we all
Wish it was fake news

April the Second
#11 / 02:04:2020

It's April the second
And the joke isn't over
Usually by now
It's the big reveal ...
Ha ha! April Fool!

Spaghetti on trees
Water in tablets
The Loch Ness Monster
Tartan paint

Not this year
Not this time

It's April the second
Hospitals under increasing pressure
Lockdown, no jobs
More deaths every day
Friends and family affected

How we long for a stupid, harmless April Fool
Instead we have this April that is cruel

Still
#12 / 03:04:2020

I found my watch today
Unworn
Stopped
Nine fifty-five
Morning or evening …
Who knows – or cares?
Time has stood still

The diary – last used three weeks ago
Days of work now cancelled
Irrelevant, unused, redundant
For the foreseeable
Time has stood still

I have no use for such as these
Unnecessary at present
Right now
As there is only "the right now"
Seconds, minutes, hours,
Days, weeks, months
They are all just … now

Time stands still
Time stands still
Time stands still
Time stands
Time stands
Time stands
Till it is time to move on

The Worst

#13 / 04:04:2020

Today was a difficult day
Quiet, eerie, solemn, edgy
Missing loved ones
Elderly parents, brothers, sisters …
Especially the children

Not children anymore
But still our babies
The house seems even quieter
Mostly that's been good, but even so …

As viral thoughts swirl viciously
Thinking the worst
The worst is starting to happen
The worst will happen to someone we know
Probably some time soon now

And here we are
Hoping that it doesn't happen to us
But if that's the best we can hope for
Can we really call that hope?

Sunshine and a Sunny Day
#14 / 05:04:2020

Sunshine and a sunny day
And it's easy to say
That things are better, everything's okay
But it's not

Sunshine and a sunny day
It's got to be good to enjoy the weather
Be together anyway
But it's not

Sunshine and a sunny day
Outside it's nice – let's ignore advice
Whatever some may say
But we can't

Sunshine and a sunny day
Surely that nullifies the threat of death
That just won't go away
But it doesn't

Selfishness, ignorance, stupidity
Unaffected by the weather and humanity
Facts remain the same
Inside you should stay
Even when there's sunshine and a sunny day

Viral

#15 / 06:04:2020

It does not discriminate
Everyone is equal
This deadly evil predator
Spreads misery and death to all

Old, young, male, female
Rich, poor, black, white, far and wide
A bus driver or a Prime Minister

Compassion is the same
It must be viral
We cannot choose those we wish well

Our hearts must reach to everyone
And if we cannot do that
We do not have compassion

And have no heart at all

A Cup of Tea and a Good Night's Sleep
#16 / 07:04:2020

When I was young
Mum would always say
A cup of tea and a good night's sleep
And everything will be okay

Sickness, bumps, every ache
A little bit of flu
And right now
I wish that this was true

I Will Not Clap for Boris
#17 / 08:04:2020

I will not clap for Boris
Although I wish him well
And when he has recovered
Perhaps he'll have discovered
The N.H.S.
Is just the best
And not something to sell

I Was Late to the Party – But You'd Already Left

for John Prine
#18 / 09:04:2020

Too many records and too little time
Folks kept telling me 'bout John Prine
If you like good songs – well he's one of the best
I was late to the party – but you'd already left

Was it just another voice, just another guitar
Just another country rock and roll star?
Well I was wrong – I must confess
I was late to the party – but you'd already left

Nothing that special? Nothing that new?
But it was so different because it was you
Humanity in every single breath
I was late to the party – but you'd already left

A song and a story and a smile on your face
You took us on the road to a different place
Heaven is somewhere – way out west
I was late to the party – but you'd already left

Humility in each melody
A living, breathing legacy
Once I was ignorant – now I say yes
I was late to the party – but you'd already left

Summer's at an end – before it's begun
God's own singer – God's own songs
Teach 'em to the angels – they can join with the rest
I was late to the party – but you'd already left

Not Walking Alone
#19 / 10:04:2020

Last night, my evening walk took me
Through fields and stiles and stiles and fields

The route I used to walk
With our beloved Springer Spaniel

Only now, I walk to the canal
Never with Max – he'd be in like a shot

I'd forgotten about the eight o'clock clap
So found myself mid-meadow

Applauding
Thinking I would be alone

Yet, echoing in the distance
I heard the ripple of spreading applause

Shouts, cheers – and even a stereo
Playing Gerry and the Pacemakers

And for someone who was walking alone
I was not

Silver Linings
#20 / 11:04:2020

The blossom seems pinker
The grass is much greener
The sunshine seems warmer
Atmosphere – cleaner

Evenings are longer
Mornings seem lighter
Daffodils yellower
Snowdrops much whiter

The sky is much bluer
Birdsong is clearer
Silence is golden
Heaven is nearer

Easter Sunday: One
#21 / 12:04:2020

Friday was in no way "Good"
Nine hundred and eighty dead
Saturday – nine hundred and seventeen

So – on Easter Sunday
When we should be thinking of
Resurrection, hope, new life

We just can't help but fear the worst

Easter Sunday: Two – Haiku
#22 / 12:04:2020

On Easter Sunday
We celebrate an empty
Tomb – but not today

An Oldie but a Goodie

for Tim Brooke Taylor
#23 / 13:04:2020

When I was young
I wanted to be Bill most of all
Long haired, funny and flared
The daft one, the wannabe rock star

Then Graeme
Corduroy boffin, brains and wit
Exotic spelling

I always thought Timbo
The wet one, the weak one
The one who didn't write the jokes

Not just an equal third
Not just a vital cog
Not just a teapot impression and Union Jack waistcoat

But a writer, performer
Funny – really funny
In his own write
I'm sorry – I just hadn't a clue

Yorkshiremen and undercover police
Nearly a Python
You ended up more than a Goodie
Smut never sounded smutty with you

You read it again
You had more than a clue
Tim Brooke Taylor
Thank you

Named

#24 / 14:04:2020

That's the lot of you – named
Hang your heads – you should be ashamed
Your actions – they should be explained
Rejecting the pay that the nurses had claimed

You cheered when their wages remained
Pitifully low, said money was strained
That a rise of this size could not be sustained
But bailing out banks is attained

Your reputations – all stained
Hospitals – broken and drained
Taking for granted all those who trained
To help the infirm, the ill and the pained

The whole sorry lot of you – named
The whole sorry lot of you – shamed
The whole sorry lot of you – blamed
… And the ten thousand pounds that you've gained

Covidiot
#25 / 15:04:2020

This ego – so mad and demented
These phrases and terms you've invented
The only new words
We wish we had heard
Is – Donald – you're – Un-President-Ed

Bad Rock Puns Warning …
#26 / 16:04:2020

Feeling lock-*Down Down*
With COVID-19
Again and again
The same routine
Living on an Island
Would be a dream

We've got …

Status Quo-rantine

Can You Hear Us Major Tom?

#27 / 17:04:2020

Captain Tom – yet your effort is major
Who would have thought
Walking round a garden a hundred times
Could capture the mood of a nation?

But it did – and it has
A heart-warming story in times of heartbreak
One hundred years old
And still able to walk around your garden

I suppose that's what you call
Ground Control, Major Tom
Your garden goal achieved
Target exceeded

You have promised to carry on
We applaud you
Can you hear us Major Tom?
Can you hear us Major Tom?

An example to us all
You have shown us where the true value lies
And who the heroes really are
We hear you Major Tom

Norman

for Norman Hunter
#28 / 18:04:2020

Even hard men cannot fight it
Even tough men cannot tackle it
You won most battles
Especially those on the pitch
Uncompromising, not one to be messed with
But not this one
Norman – you've been hunted

Your face on my Esso World Cup Coins
More than a name on a football card
Winner, champion
And alleged "biter of legs"
We may have called you dirty
But we'd have had you in our team
In a flash, our general
But, Norman – you have been hunted

More than just a hard man
More than just an enforcer
Vital cog in a winning team
Because of your reputation
Ability was overlooked
The skill and the steel
A real player's player

This time – unlike with Frannie Lee –
You could not fight back
This time
The opposition was too strong
And you lost

And just like many others lost
You are someone's son, husband
Father, granddad, loved one, friend …

And they have lost too

Norman Hunter – one of a kind
Another good one gone

Cornflakes
#29 / 19:04:2020

This morning
I had Cornflakes for breakfast
At home – for the first time
In many a year

And it reminded me of
A thousand childhood breakfasts
Around a family kitchen table
Where we were allowed to add
A spoonful of sugar (only one, mind)

But mum and dad would never, ever
Ever buy Frosties

So – this morning
I had Cornflakes
With a spoonful – and a bit – of sugar
And, just for a few minutes
Life tasted a little bit sweeter

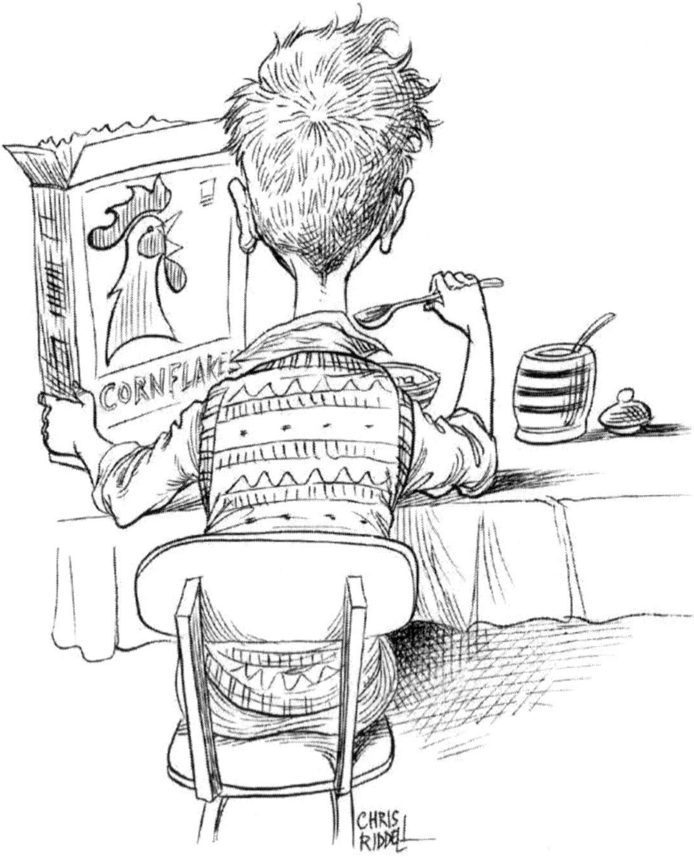
CORNFLAKES
CHRIS RIDDELL

Leaders Failing to Lead Us

#30 / 20:04:2020

It's coming to light that meetings were missed
COVID-19 – not top of your list
If this is true, the fact is just this
Leaders failing to lead us

Lessons not learned from countries elsewhere
Not taking note of what's happening there
Where is the diligence? Where is the care?
Leaders failing to lead us

It now seems that those in authority
Did not see this as a priority
The reality – for you and for me
Leaders failing to lead us

Underprepared – when warnings were clear
Blinkered and blasé – it can't happen here
Under-invested for many a year
Leaders failing to lead us

Not recognising a global pandemic
You don't have to be a great academic
But you are Dad's Army saying "Don't panic"
Leaders failing to lead us

Too little too late when lives are now lost
Too little too late – we're counting the cost
Too little too late – simply because
Leaders failing to lead us

It may have been "unpredictable" or
"Unprecedented" – but we can't ignore
You could have and should have done so much more
Leaders failing to lead us

Not a Good Time for My Business
#31 / 21:04:2020

Times they are hard, the times they are a-changing
The times that we live in are times that are strange in
My work possibilities need rearranging
Not a good time for my business

Pickings once rich – now they are nil
COVID-19 – with everyone ill
I cannot depend on public goodwill
Not a good time for my business

My night shifts have ended – left all alone
No-one gets out – they all stay at home
I cannot get in and take what you own
Not a good time for my business

Steeling myself for tough times ahead
Steeling myself – I'm now in the red
I'd steal from myself but there's nowt in my shed
Not a good time for my business

My livelihood has been taken away
I'd do the taking – but not today
Crime doesn't pay – true what they say
Not a good time for my business

No government help for someone like me
Usually me gets something for free
Not a good time for thieving and crime
Not a good time for my business

Nobody Famous Died Today

#32 / 22:04:2020

No beloved entertainer
Or footballer who used to play
No-one from the television
No-one famous died today

No singer of a favourite song
The one from all our yesterdays
No-one royal, no-one rich
No-one famous died today

Nurses, doctors, health workers
Front line folk on lower pay
Care assistants, helpers out
They're the ones who died today

Grandma Joan, Granddad Bill
Uncle Frank, Auntie May
A brother, sister, mum and dad
Important people died today

Someone special – every one
Taken – not just passed away
Those loved most – lost and gone
Too many that have died today

Too many every day

I Seem to Be Agreeing with Somebody Called Piers
#33 / 23:04:2020

These times are getting stranger – and stranger by the day
Where once I questioned everything that you would do and say
What's worrying and stranger still is now that it appears
I seem to be agreeing with somebody called Piers

Once smug and self-satisfied with ego so inflated
You almost seem respected where once you seemed so hated
A journalist investigates – after all these years!
I seem to be agreeing with somebody called Piers

Asking all the questions that are needing to be asked
P.P.E. and testing and where are gowns and masks?
And why oh why the government is so far in arrears
I seem to be agreeing with somebody called Piers

That voice that was annoying seems now a people's voice
Shouting what we'd say if we had the means and choice
Raising our frustrations, empathising with our fears
I seem to be agreeing with somebody called Piers

Failures with mass gatherings and the need to be decisive
Hypocrisy and dithering – your questions now incisive
Who'd have thought that after all – you'd have such good ideas
I seem to be agreeing with somebody called Piers

Once I would be wishing you'd donate a vital organ
But now it's somewhat different with a different Mr Morgan
It's weird that we think you're great and do not grate our ears
I seem to be agreeing
Believing it is seeing

And despite your reputation
You are a human being
So I'll tip my hat, raise a glass and quietly say "cheers"
Blimey – I'm agreeing with somebody called Piers

Thank Our Lucky Stars
#34 / 24:04:2020

It's forever in the news 'coz we've got the lockdown blues
Dragging us down further – deeper in the dump
And while this virus is a curse, just think – it could be worse
We could be in America - with Trump

Pandemical deniers say the medicals are liars
And it's like a strain of flu or just like mumps
They ignore the facts of science and their sole reliance
Are the words and the actions of the Trumps

This land that's of the free riddled with stupidity
Re-open all the shops, fight the economic slump
Demanding liberty – ME – ME – ME
Just like the example of a certain Mr Trump

The president's suggestion is injection and digestion
Of disinfectant with a single pump
And salvation for the nation with UV radiation
The wisdom from the expert Dr Trump

Whose limited ideas have access to all ears
Loud enough to make you stop and jump
Ignores the scientific, cannot be specific
The general ignorance of Major Trump

Patriotic, idiotic, chronically psychotic
A despot who is spouting from his rump
Ignorance seems bliss – but the problem is
Lots of people listening to Trump

The future sure ain't bright – it's orange and it's shite
With this cranially challenged brainless chump
But the positive we've got is we're here and we're not
Living in America with Trump

Far beyond a joke that ordinary folk
Cannot see beyond this lard-ass lump
So thank our lucky stars that his government's not ours
And we are not misled by Donald Trump

Saturday Night Lockdown Blockbusters
#35 / 25:04:2020

Imagine what if
A boy with a quiff
A hero from Belgium that we know

Had a Reservoir Dog
Called Snowy because
It's …

Tintin Quarantino

Priti Obvious, Priti Vacant
#36 / 26:04:2020

Shoplifting – at an all-time low
Tell us something we don't know

Football hooligans – they're down too
Burglaries – well, who knew?

Fewer car crashes this year
The M25 is nice and clear

Pretty clear that there's a link
Priti, please – stop and think

Overheard in a Supermarket Queue – Two Metres Apart

(He was talking loudly by the way)
#37 / 27:04:2020

Stay home
Stay safe
Two metres apart
Take note of the guidelines my dears

Social distancing …
No problem
Me and the wife have done it for years

COVID-19 Killed the Radio Star … and Other Bad Pop Puns

(You have been warned…)
#38 / 28:04:2020

Everybody Wants to Cure the World
Livin' on a Prayer at best
One Vaccination Under a Groove
With …

Quaran-Tina Turner's Simply the Test

On the Passing of Grandparents and Great Grandparents
#39 / 29:04:2020

Day by day by day by day
Silently, they slip away

Our ever-present everydays
Those constants in our family ways

No last goodbyes that we can say
No final prayers that we can pray

No favourite music we can play
One last time – our yesterdays

No holding hands, just where they lay
No hug, pretending it's okay

The distance that we have to stay
We cannot keep this force at bay

This lonely death, the price to pay
This generation – lost and grey

Day by day by day by day by day
Silently, they slip away

The Only Thing That's Doctored …
#40 / 30:04:2020

A billion items – all supplied
To hospitals – nationwide
But the truth is more than this
And what's really happened is
Each individual item counts
To constitute these vast amounts
Camouflaged statistics while the problem's getting bigger
The only thing that's doctored are the figures

Count one single glove – not two
One single paper towel – it's true
One apron made from polythene
Not much to fight COVID-19
Not vital items – P.P.E.
See this and you must agree
Ill-prepared, ill-thought out – a government that slumbers
The only thing that's doctored are the numbers

Pandemic warnings – all ignored
Stock not stockpiled, bought or stored
Can it be too much to ask
For simple things like gowns or masks?
If other governments could see
Potential problems why can't we?
Too late with too little while this virus still attacks
The only thing that's doctored are the facts

A government that we elect
Then has a duty to protect
A duty for decisive action
Not kneejerk copy-cat reaction

A duty then to plan and care
Due diligence to be prepared
For possible and probables and not remain aloof
The only thing that's doctored is the truth

These troubled times we live in are the proof
The only thing protected is the truth

At Least the Rain Will Keep the Idiots In
#41 / 01:05:2020

Hasn't it been lovely weather for this time of year?
But now the sunshine's gone and the drizzle's here
We live in hope that the sun will soon be back again
But at least the rain will keep the idiots in

Much too wet to walk that extra mile or two
Nowhere near dry enough for a barbecue
It's gone and put a dampener on family gatherings
But at least the rain will keep the idiots in

I'd rather see two or three putting up umbrellas
Than a bench with a bunch of chatting laughing fellas
Or a group of gossips, yapping, giggling
At least this rain will keep the idiots in

All this lockdown boredom is leading to resistance
Morons getting blasé about their social distance
If we ignore it all it's a battle we won't win
But at least the rain will keep the idiots in

There's calls for personal freedom and our civil rights
It's got to be for all of us – and even then it might …
Might just be that some of us live through COVID-19
But at least the rain will keep the idiots in

It's better that we don't get wetter
Follow guidelines to the letter
And if it has to rain all year then we'll take it on the chin
At least it keeps the idiots all in

The Satanic Versus …
#42 / 02:05:2020

All the comings and the goings
Nothing that he isn't knowing
All the time his power growing
The dark lord sat in waiting
In the shadows at the back
Don't be fooled by his anorak
Dominic's on the attack
Like the power of Satan

Machiavellian puller of strings
Lurking, furtive in the wings
Plays the tune the puppet sings
Do not be mistaken
Sly and slimy, wily, weaselly
He'll hoodwink you oh so easily
Behind those glasses, scheming evilly
The darkened soul of Satan

Part hobgoblin, part dementor
Torturer and then tormentor
Herd mentality presenter
There is no escaping
From the one who's heard to say
If old ones die – then that's the way
The economy must be okay
The pawn that's born of Satan

Compassion, hope and empathy
Not in his vocabulary
All the herd mentality
Is the stance he's taken
Wouldn't touch him with a barge pole
Like to hit him with a large pole
Then chuck him down a really large hole
Bury him with Satan

The name that always comes up
When the Devil's mass debating
Demonic Comings – sums you up
You are … the spawn of Satan

Solace

(After listening to Chuck Prophet's 'Strings in the Temple')
#43 / 03:05:2020

Today I didn't watch the news
Instead
I found solace in music
Strings sing and take me away
Cause goose-bumps to rise

Transported elsewhere
Real life forgotten in those moments
While notes transcend reality

Songs I knew and loved
Violins and strings
Love and hope in art
Solace in these things

Tomorrow – maybe a much-loved book
A painting, a psalm
A prayer, a poem
But these will give you solace
If we but give them time

Hand in Hand

#44 / 04:05:2020

Once death has touched you
It holds you hand forever

Frozen fingers squeeze and squeeze
Until you are numb

Skeletal bones grind
Against the very skin of life itself

And while that life is ever-present
So, now, is that death

A circle, intertwined
Alpha, omega and all that lies between

Tight and cold right now
But it never lets you go

Time may loosen that grip
But forever now you are connected

Once death has touched you
It holds your hand forever

Punk Rock Moustache

for Dave Greenfield
#45 / 05:05:2020

Punks didn't have moustaches
Punks didn't play the keyboards
But you were The Stranglers
And didn't care

Punks didn't have centre parting-ed longer hair
Punks didn't play longer songs
But you were The Stranglers
And didn't care

Punks didn't work with old jazz musicians
Or cover songs like *Walk on By*
But you were The Stranglers
And didn't care

Moustaches and keyboards
Always more than a punk
You were the sound of The Stranglers
And we did care

Here to Stay Each Day

#46 / 06:05:2020

No-one grates your cheese greater
I'm your perfect toastie maker
Magic with a baked potato
Here to stay each day

First tea in the morning brew-er
List ticker, bidding do-er
Be we rich or be we poor
Here to stay each day

I will run your perfect bath
Wash the pots, cut the grass
Occasionally – make you laugh
Here to stay each day

It may be 24/7
Doesn't always feel like heaven
But that's just the way we're living
Here to stay each day

Isolated – but together
It won't always be forever
Here we are – come whatever
Here to stay each day

Fighting Talk
#47 / 07:05:2020

You cannot wrestle a virus
You cannot hit it back
A bug is not a mugger
With a random chance attack

You can't punch a pandemic
You cannot strangle a strain
You cannot grapple a germ
Retaliate vee pain

You cannot fight a battle
With a force that can't be seen
Fighting talk – useless words
Against COVID-19

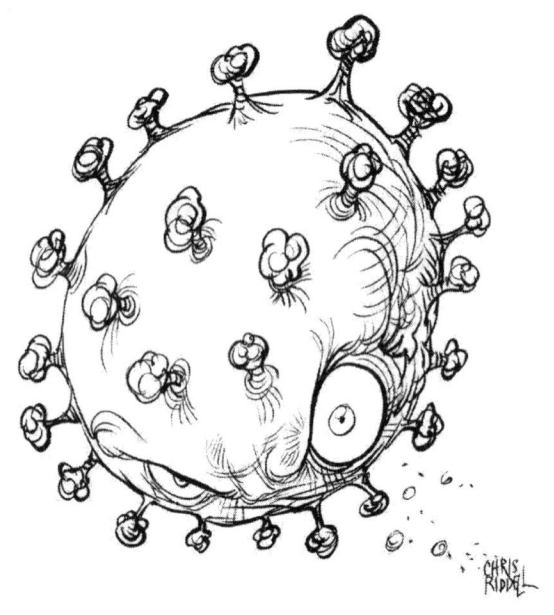

These Could Be the Good Old Days
#48 / 08:05:2020

These are the days
We will remember forever
If we are the lucky ones

Just like elderly relatives
Always mentioned the war
Our children will always remember "Lockdown"

They will laugh about toilet rolls
Hand sanitiser, the importance of pasta
And how much DIY, gardening and exercise they did

They may even say the phrase
"Ah – the good old days
… when we actually had a National Health Service"

They may remember these
As times when strangers reached out
And we saw the best in people

They may even remember this
As when times changed – for the better
And we started to value each other
Key workers became the ordinary heroes
Politicians became accountable
And life became more important than mere economics

These might one day
Turn out to be "The Good Old Days"
If we can but learn

V.E. Day Celebrations
#49 / 09:05:2020

In these times, is this a day for celebration?
Is it ever a time for celebration?
How can we celebrate a victory
In the face of so much loss?

For, if we celebrate, then we glory
In the deaths of the "so called enemy"
Not the henchmen of Hitler
The co-conspirators of evil

But the everyday soldiers, airmen and sailors
Placed squarely in the firing line
The young forced into a uniform
Purely on the circumstances of birth, time and geography

Once you pass down the ranks
Privates, civilians … there is no difference
We are all the same
We are all losers

And yet, we cannot help but be moved
By bravery, sacrifice and all the prices paid
As they made their mark in our history
And changed our lives

And for that, yes, we must remember, always
We must salute them and be proud
Proud of their dignity
Proud of the peace they won

Not celebration
But true commemoration

Another Day, Another Headline, Another Poem
#50 / 10:05:2020

Another day, another headline
Another day, another poem

Let's keep going
This plan is working

Mixed metaphors muddy and confuse
Road maps and menu options

But the question remains
What "plan" is that?

What planet are you on
If you think this is actually working?

More clichés
More empty rhetoric

We have to keep going
We have no choice

Same old words
Much like this poem

Haiku for Little Richard
#51 / 10:05:2020

If Noddy Holder
Says he wants to be like you
Then you are the king

A Mess of Contradictions
#52 / 11:05:2020

Tally ho! It's back to work
Stay safe and stay alert
Understood?
Clear as mud

Stay Alert Boris
#53 / 11:05:2020

If we are to stay alert then it surely can't be wrong
To assume that you have been alert – right from day one

The facts would beg to differ, the dates don't really work
Too much un-noticed and not done if you had been alert

Twenty fourth and twenty ninth of Jan and Feb the fifth
Another on the twelfth – Cobra meetings missed

February the thirteenth – nothing at all
For a European Leaders' Conference Call

February fourteenth – Valentine
Holiday time so everything's fine

Eighteenth – another Cobra missed
Like COVID-19 just doesn't exist

And so it goes on and goes on and goes on
Emails are "lost" and chances are gone

You could follow the lead of leaders elsewhere
Take the advice from the knowledge they share

Learn from mistakes that others are making
You're too busy sleeping to think about waking

I'm no politician – no "so called" expert
But …you cannot stay alert if you've never been alert

Alert to the dangers, alert to the facts
Alert to the truth, alert to act

Staying Alert, Staying Alert –
are the words you'd have us sing

But it's *Staying Alive* that we need –
your words don't mean a thing

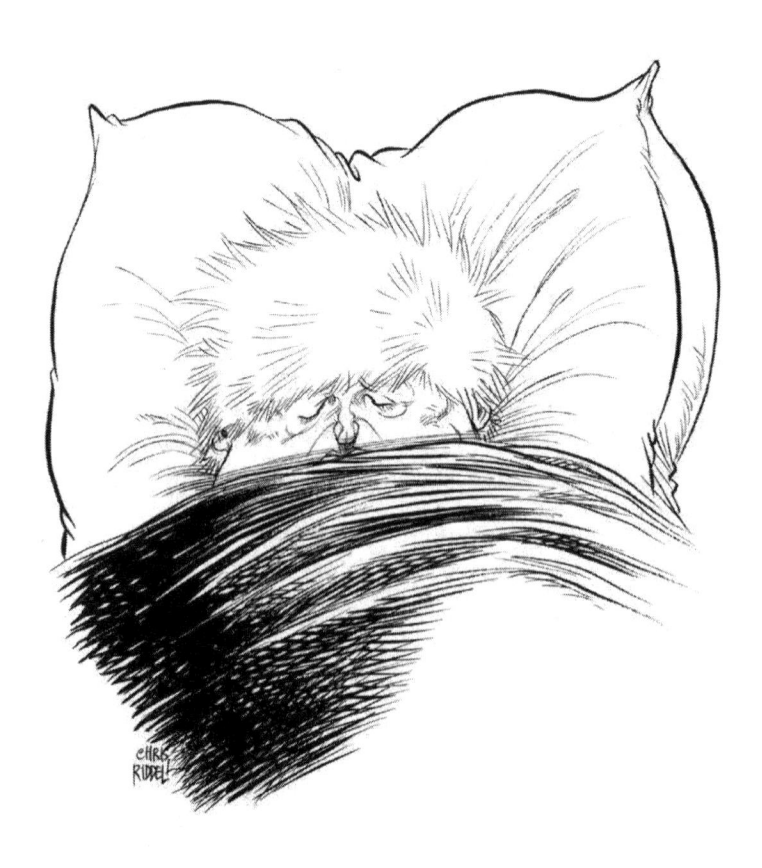

Over to You

#54 / 12:05:2020

Stay Home and Save Lives – this message was clear
But because it's not working we're living in fear
That you might find out we could have done more
Than watching that horse bolt from our door

The plans have all changed – the trap has been set
The goal posts are moved – our cleverest yet
We've done what we can – we've done what we ought
So we're throwing the ball back into your court

You want us to move – you want us to act
We know you need work – exploiting that fact
We know you want "normal" – you're sick of the wait
So it's over to you to take up the bait

We've got a new slogan – to guide and advise
Carefully worded so we're not telling lies
A catchphrase, a jingle, a tagline so twee
A phrase that's so vague – you can't disagree

This piffle and waffle of meaningless phrases
Road maps and menus and nebulous phases
All this rhetoric, all this pretence
Of old fashioned British good common sense

If you're not careful – if you don't stay alert
If you contract the virus when you have to work
Then that is your choice – to do what you do
It's not down to us - so it's now up to you

Schools Can't Cope with an Outbreak of Nits, but COVID-19 … Dead Easy
#55 / 13:05:2020

Wash the pencils, gel the pens
Wipe the whiteboards twice and then
Bleach the toilets, mop the floors
Disinfect the corridors
Scrub the benches, clean the chairs
And bannisters on all the stairs
Ensure tables are pristine
Sanitise the plasticine
Cleanse the cutlery each day
Every plastic dinner tray
Every handle, every door
Do it once and then twice more
Move each desk before you start
Keep the pupils well apart
Wet-wipe books on all the shelves
Make the kids play by themselves
Wash the pencils, gel the pens
Then it's time to start again
Do this and more and I am guessing
You won't have time to teach a lesson

You Cannot Social Distance in a School
#56 / 14:05:2020

If adults cannot understand the concept and the fear
How can we expect the under-tens to hear
And act upon the nuances of this bad idea?
It may be in existence but you can't enforce the rule
You cannot social distance in a school

The nature of the classroom and the strength of education
Is unity, community and co-operation
How can that be possible in this situation?
It may be in existence but you can't enforce the rule
You cannot social distance in a school

Let's take the youngest children, remove them from their home
Where they've been safe and sound and make them sit alone
Where they can see the other lonely children on their own
It may be in existence but you can't enforce the rule
You cannot social distance in a school

You cannot tell a child that they cannot play with friends
Or that they have to work alone until the lesson ends
Is this the message that you really want to send?
It may be in existence but you can't enforce the rule
You cannot social distance in a school

We hear the old cliché ... "good old common sense"
But where's the common sense in this ill-thought out pretence?
It's stupid and it's dangerous and there is no defence
It may be in existence but you can't enforce the rule
You cannot social distance in a school

It's "economics first" – or stubborn as a mule
For only the resistance and persistence of a fool
Would suggest this ignorance and policy so cruel
You cannot social distance
It is non-existent
You cannot social distance in a school

Let Our Teachers Be Heroes
#57 / 15:05:2020

The headlines scream in black and white
It's in the papers – it must be right
They're front line workers – so fight the fight
Our teachers have always been heroes

This battle language, war of words
Means we're shaken and we're stirred
But hides the truth that can't be heard
Our teachers have always been heroes

They say the reasons staff don't act is
Militancy but the fact is
Safety first and good practice
Our teachers have always been heroes

Health and safety, risk assessment
That should be the first investment
Doesn't matter what the press meant
Our teachers have always been heroes

When the all clear time arrives
That's the time for schools to thrive
Until then let's stay alive
Our teachers have always been heroes

All these clichés that you shout
Ill-prepared and ill-thought out
The poison and the lies you spout
Our teachers have always been heroes

Education – Education – Differentiation
#58 / 16:05:2020

Public schools – in September
State schools open in June
If it's not the same for everyone
Then right now is too soon

Public schools – well, not quite yet
State schools – yes, now is the time
That tells us what we want to know
Where priorities lie

Public schools – keep the gates closed
State – throw open the doors
One rule for the rich …

Mr Hancock's Half Hour
#59 / 16:05:2020

You want "complete transparency"
In everything you say and do
You've got it, Mr Hancock
We can all see right through you

Blackbird on a Sunday Morning

#60 / 17:05:2020

The blackbird sings on fresh cut grass
With notes the angels understand
Heaven's song and evensong – a mass
An ode to this green pleasant land

A simple bird, the blackbird sings
And lightens every heart and every soul
Pure and shrill – he is the king
This song of songs, this purest gold

We're All in This Together

#61 / 17:05:2020

So, fill the House of Commons
Cram every seat and bench
Every nook and cranny
Let ministers of all persuasions
Stand shoulder to shoulder
Let our elected representatives
Represent us as they stare closely into each other's eyes
Let the chambers echo with words
Let speeches be punctuated with jeers
And coughs, cheers, high-fives, even the odd snore
Let there be standing room only
Let every member be present
Breathing the same hot air
Together

And when all this is done
Then and only then
Will we heed your words of bravery
And follow your leadership and example
Then will we congregate in classrooms
Fill our factory floors
Overflow the offices
Cheer on our football teams
And get back to normal

When you all go back to work
Then so shall we
Especially as we are all in this together
Good old-fashioned common sense isn't it?

Are You Sitting Comfortably? Good, We Can Begin

(Text for an unpublished and unpublishable picture book)
#62 / 18:05:2020

Hello boys and girls
This is Michael
Say hello to Michael

See Michael sitting alone
See his hair – all neatly brushed and combed
See Michael polish his spectacles
See Michael's lovely suit and straight tie
Smart Michael

See Michael try to smile
See how difficult it is for Michael
See his lips try to move
But Michael looks like a reptile
Poor Michael

Michael loves to read
Some of his best friends are books
See him turn the pages
Read – read – read – read – read
Clever Michael

Michael thinks he likes science too
He talks to people who are cleverer than him
But Michael doesn't listen
Because Michael thinks he is cleverer than them
See Michael cover his ears
Silly Michael

But Michael is strong
Very strong

Michael thinks he knows best
Even when his clever friends don't agree
So Michael carries on
Brave Michael

Michael knows lots of words
He likes to use them and show off
Michael likes the sound of his own voice
So Michael carries on talking
All the time
Loud Michael

Michael says things that aren't true
Michael knows they aren't true
But still he says them
Because Michael thinks he knows best
Naughty Michael

Look boys and girls
You can tell when Michael is telling fibs
See Michael's mouth moving
Every time it moves, he tells naughty fibs and lies
Bad Michael

But Michael doesn't mind
Michael doesn't care
Michael doesn't care at all
Very bad Michael

Do you believe in monsters, boy and girls?
Not all monsters have sharp horns
Big teeth and nasty claws
Some have neat hair, spectacles
And lovely neat ties
Monstrous Michael

He Was

#63 / 19:05:2020

He was an amazing man
One of the best
One of my favourite people

He was wonderful and caring
One of the loveliest
We were lucky to have known him

He was lovely
Truly a gentleman
And a true gentleman

He was delightful and amazing
A hero in every way
Always a good friend

He was special
A massive heart
One of the nicest men I've ever met

Scrolling down comments
Reading cards
Our eyes fill up

Not just because of the truth
But because of the word
"Was"

Aftermath

#64 / 20:05:2020

The birds sang
The sun shone
In the midst of life there is death

Social distancing – maybe
But together we gathered
Together we mourned

A fireman's guard of honour
A fitting tribute, respect and integrity
We all saluted you

Heartfelt words and memories resonate
Much loved music fills the air
As we remembered … remembered

Love divine – all loves excelling
The Lord is my shepherd
The comfort of faith and prayer

Wood, brass and dust
Flowers, soil and marble
Tears, love and goodbyes

All the clichés present
But clichés are the truth
Worlds turned upside down

The birds shone
The sun sang
In the midst of death there was life

You

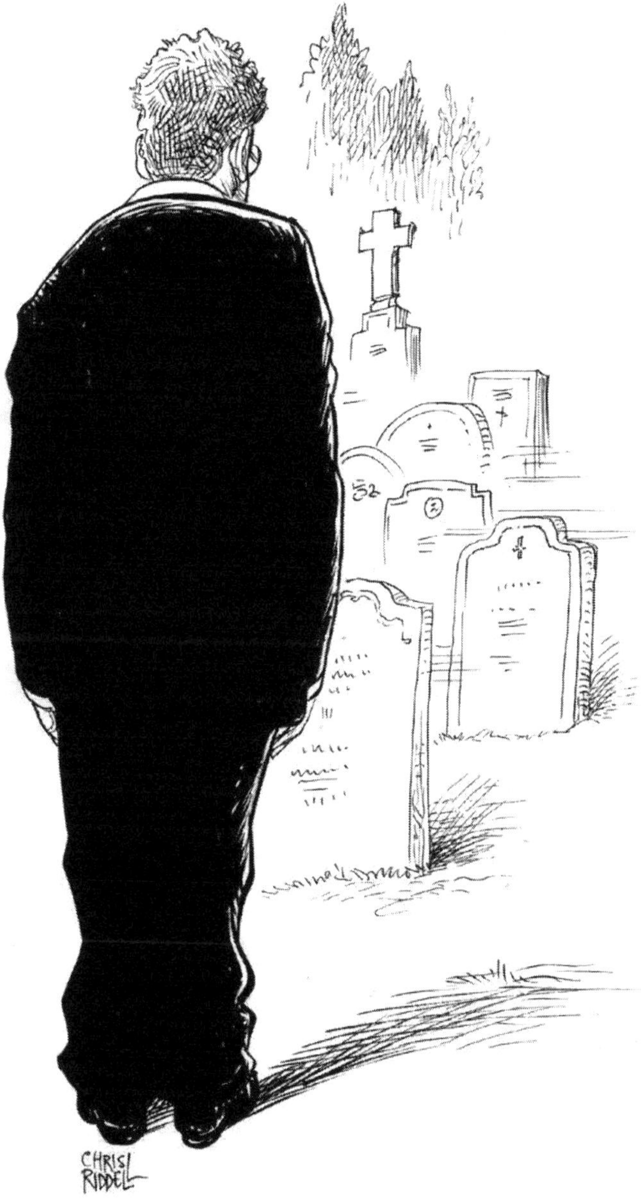
CHRIS RIDDELL

Missed
#65 / 21:05:2020

I hit the post, the ball bounced out
Let's call it a goal anyway
Number nineteen in the top forty
Call it number one, well waddayasay?

I owe you a pound, here's eighty pee
Let's say you're paid in full
I drew my bow, the arrow flew
Grazed the white – let's call it bull

You promised us a target
But your numbers don't add up
You promised us a target
And now it's "ifs" and "buts"

A hundred-thousand tests a day
By the time we reach the first of May
Not there by a long chalk
But hey, it's okay

Because you tried, you really tried
You said you've done your level best
Because you're there or thereabouts
Let's say you've passed the test

Just like those who had exams
A-levels, G.C.S.E.
Now they can have an A
When once predicted C

Nowhere near your SATs?
Never mind – you've passed
Under these new rules
No-one need come last

Richard Coles, Anne Widdecombe
Strictly King and Queen
Eddie the Eagle – gold
Champions League for every team

To be pragmatic with mathematics
It's either wrong or right
Numbers do not lie
It's there in black and white

You invented this number
No spin – and no twist
You set your very own targets
… And still you missed

Too
#66 / 22:05:2020

Too little
Too late
Too trite
Too vague

Too muddled
Too often
Too mixed
Too casual

Too few
Too sensible
Too numerous
Too selfish

Too flippant
To care
Too stupid
To think

Too long
To wait
Too short
Term view

Too great
A risk
Too much
To lose

Too many
Will die

Too true

Comings and Goings
#67 / 23:05:2020

So … surprise, surprise
One rule for you
And a different one for us

You gave advice to the nation
You set guidelines for the general public

For others

The arrogance of power
The ignorance of responsibility

How can we trust you now?
If we ever did

Others have resigned for similar acts
Of defiance and stupidity

No doubt you won't

But we all know you should
Like you knew you shouldn't travel

Two hundred and fifty miles
But you did

Cummings and going
Let's hope so

Not So Very Long Ago
#68 / 24:05:2020

Not so very long ago
A politician was derided, demeaned and demonised
For wearing a coat deemed shabby
And a tie not properly knotted

Now we have a Prime Minister
Incapable of brushing his own hair in a tidy manner
And an adviser in a hoody, beanie hat, untucked shirt
And coat that could be deemed shabby

No derision, demeaning, demonisation

Recently, another politician was accused of
Having a field
To ridicule, spin and slander

Today we have
Someone who made the rules
Then broke the rules – deliberately

There are lies, untruths, cover-ups
Inconsistencies – to say the very least – abound
The hypocrisy of all being in this together

No derision, demeaning or demonisation

"Maverick ally" says The Daily Mail
And for once they are
Almost right

Maverick
A liar

Meanwhile, in Other News …
Arctic Penguin Poop Gives Off Laughing Gas

#69 / 25:05:2020

You can stay at home or stay alert
These messages – irrational
Just what is social distancing?
Confusion that is national
The death toll rises higher
From what has come to pass
Meanwhile – in other news
Arctic penguin poop gives off laughing gas

Well, Dominic's "responsible"
And "acted legally"
The "instincts of a father"
With "integrity"
So says Boris Johnson
In a briefing brash and crass
Meanwhile – in other news
Arctic penguin poop gives off laughing gas

Spin the lies and twist the truth
Is that all you do?
You want complete transparency
We see through all of you
Undermining sacrifices
Playing loose and fast
Meanwhile – in other news
Arctic penguin poop gives off laughing gas

Disregard for guidelines
They sought to implement
One rule for the rulers
Is what they really meant

Double-standards, double-talk
Lies and lies en masse
Meanwhile – in other news
Arctic penguin poop gives off laughing gas

Even your supporters scream
"What planet are you on?"
You must have failed when The Mail
Thinks you have done wrong
You cannot do the right thing
You can't show any class
Meanwhile – in other news
Arctic penguin poop gives off laughing gas

A penguin's defecation
Leads to gaseous emissions
Like the proclamations of
A minister's decisions
But it's no laughing matter
When the opposite is true
When Boris Johnson talks
We all can smell the poo

We might see your mouth move
But you're talking through your ass
Meanwhile – in other news
Arctic penguin poop gives off laughing gas

A straw that breaks the camel's back
Well, maybe this is it
When Boris Johnson talks
We all can smell the shit

This Poem is True
#70 / 26:05:2020

This poem is true
It contains words that all exist in the dictionary
These words are not fake or false
So, this poem is true

All the words in this poem are real
No words have been invented
They are words we all know
So, this poem is true

No words have been mispronounced
All are spelt correctly
They are all every day, reasonable words
So, this poem is true

Words like "family", "childcare" and "sickness"
Words we can easily agree with
Words we can all relate to

Words like "worried" and "wife"
"Car" and "castle"
Good examples of alliteration

This poem uses real words
But does not tell the full story
Because this poem is sometimes forgetful
Some words have been left out

But, nevertheless, this poem is true
In that all the words here are real words
This poem chooses its words very carefully

It does not use words we have all been using
Like "responsibility", "all in this together"
Or "stay at home"

This poem will not apologise
For this glaring omission
And why should it?

You have read all the words
And these words are real
So, this poem is true

This poem knows the difference
Between honesty and truth
So, this poem is being very careful

No Regrets
#71 / 27:05:2020

This story will not go just yet
But there are no regrets
Oblivious to those upset
But there are no regrets

It may be tricky and complex
But guidelines are the ones you set
Not the spirit we expect
Or the standards we accept
But there are no regrets

An own goal in the home team net
Like a jelly not quite set
Or shifting sand that's soaking wet
An example that you didn't set
But there are no regrets

The strangest facts that you select
The dots are there but don't connect
It doesn't even feel correct
Lost the plots and lost respect
But there are no regrets

Just what is it that you don't get?

No regrets that we thought twice
Followed government advice
Made a personal sacrifice
Isolated – paid the price

No regrets you undermined
A national mood that tried to find
A way through this that's helpful, kind
Ignorant? Or are you blind?

What do you not understand?
What makes you so underhand?
You give us cause to wonder and
Question why you're in demand
When your fiction's unbelievable
Logic inconceivable
But you think it's achievable
That your position is retrievable

Arrogant and bulletproof
Condescending and aloof
Would it hurt to tell the truth?
Prove you've not a cloven hoof
And still you've no regrets?
Still you've no regrets?
Elite and heartless hypocrites
Move on – no regrets

I Think That I'm in Love with Emily Maitlis

#72 / 28:05:2020

We all live in troubled times, days unprecedented
Isolating, hibernating, going quite demented
But if there is a lining that is silver then it's this
I think that I'm in love with Emily Maitlis

The downside is the doom and gloom, the stories in the press
Political shenanigans, an ever-growing mess
But if there is an upside, then the upside is
I'm seeing so much more of Emily Maitlis

A woman of intelligence and blessed with common sense
Like a knife through butter re the government's intents
Dominic's short comings, the spin, the lies, the twist
That's why I think we are in love with Emily Maitlis

She says just what we're thinking and says it honestly
Yet reprimanded and removed by the BBC
Views right here on Newsnight – so how can they dismiss
The queen who's been upon our screen – Emily Maitlis

Emily's no enemy – the voice of truth for you and me
Emily – the remedy – is plain and clear for all to see
Newsnight doesn't feel quite right – the presence that we miss
That's why we all love you – Emily Maitlis

Impartiality
#73 / 29:05:2020

In
The
Interests
Of
Impartiality
This
Poem
Will
Take
A
Neutral
Stance
And
Show
No
Political
Bias
Left
Or
Right
Furthermore
It
Will
Not
Mention
By
Name
Any
Public
Figures

Deemed
To
Have
Questions
Hanging
Over
Their
Suitability
For
Public
Service
This
Poem
Is
Perfect
For
Newsnight

Civic Duty
#74 / 29:05:2020

I'll gladly do my civic duty
And not visit castles of natural beauty

A Happy Song for Us to Sing to Celebrate the Fact We are No. 1 in Europe … in the Death Toll Charts

#75 / 30:05:2020

The sun has got his hat on
Hip – hip – hip - hooray

We're not down in lockdown
And everything's okay

Things are back to normal
And COVID's gone away

Cos … the sun has got his hat on
And six of us can play

Dominic and Boris
Both have had their say

Even though they both should go
Both of them will stay

The sun has got his hat on
Hip – hip – hip – hooray

Yes, the sun has got his hat on
And we're coming out to play

Fifteen in a classroom
It's the perfect way

For moving on and staying safe
Let us not delay

The sun has got his hat on
Hip – hip – hip – hooray

The sun has got his hat on
And it's barbecues today

Down by the Riverbank
#76 / 31:05:2020

It was good to get out
More than good, great

A walk down by the riverbank
Sunshine, shorts, shades

The serenade of birdsong
And the perfect breeze

A few families sat in groups
Children splashed and laughed

A dog couldn't resist the lure of water
Neither could two teenagers

Who jumped fearlessly
Then couldn't get out quick enough

A comical crow picked and pecked
At a crisp packet on the riverbank

And I remembered childhood days
Bike rides and blue skies

The fascination of water
However cold, green and slimy

And family picnics on riverbanks
Meat paste sandwiches, diluted squash and budget crisps

And when it was time to go mum and dad
Would make sure we packed up all our litter

And any other bits of rubbish
Before we went home

Down by the riverbank
With the sunshine, the breeze, the birdsong

And crisp packets and cans

Prayer for the First Day of School
#77 / 01:06:2020

God bless the teachers in this new test
God bless the children as they try their best
God bless the parents – now worried alone
God bless all those who kept theirs at home

Give them all wisdom, kindness and strength
Patience and thoughtfulness, good common sense
May there be laughter, may there be fun
As they work together to get this thing done

But most of all Lord
In this new unknown
Keep them all safe
And bring them all home

When the First Child Dies in School
#78 / 01:06:2020

When the first child dies in school
Then will you say that this was the right time?

When someone's son or daughter is lost
Because of an infection passed on in the playground
Will you still stand by your call
For schools to have opened so soon?

Or will you blame the teachers for dereliction of duty
And not following procedures?

Health. Safety. Life.
More important than grades right now

Let the teachers get it right
As they always have

The Truth That's in The Bible is Lost Because of You

#79 / 02:06:2020

You give God a bad name every time you talk about him
You make it so easy – to think of life without him
You are the perfect reason – for everyone to doubt him
I cannot see Jesus in anything you do
The truth that's in The Bible is lost because of you

You glory in the story of riches stored in heaven
Redemption and salvation and sins that are forgiven
But then ignore so many more and the poverty they live in
You say you care and offer prayer – but that is nothing new
The truth that's in The Bible is lost because of you

You talk of love thy neighbour when your heart is full of hate
No time to feed the hungry when you've so much on your plate
You say good things will come – to those who pray and wait
Condescending, patronising, blinkered point of view
The truth that's in The Bible is lost because of you

Hypocrisy your middle name – you spell it differently
You think it's P-R-I-N-C-I-P and L and E
The sermon on the mount is a page you didn't see
Salvation is for everyone and not the chosen few
The truth that's in The Bible is lost because of you

Your narrow-minded views mean that your heart's forever closed
Compassion is a foreign word for those less indisposed
Empathy and sympathy – both undiagnosed
If faith has a sticking point – you must be the glue
The truth that's in The Bible is lost because of you

You talk of being godly – when plainly you are not
Instead pride and prejudice are qualities you've got
Judge that ye be not judged – something you forgot
The fact that you are lying is the only thing that's true
The truth that's in The Bible is lost because of you

You say that you believe but you don't understand
That faith and compassion go hand in hand in hand
Your excuse for doing nothing is that God had got it planned
You think you know what's right but you haven't got a clue
The truth that's in The Bible is lost because of you

You think that being holy is silence and respect
But silence is a wholly inappropriate concept
Sometimes you've got to shout against the violence and neglect
Change is like your library books – too long overdue
The truth that's in The Bible is lost because of you

You read that Jesus washes sins away whiter than white
But whiter than white is not a phrase we need tonight
Hiding from the truth in a White House with no light
Darkness and division and tear gas on cue
The truth that's in The Bible is lost because of you

Take the Knee
#80 / 03:06:2020

Solidarity
Take the knee

Equality
Take the knee

Democracy
Take the knee

Unity
Take the knee

Community
Take the knee

Empathy
Take the knee

Humility
Take the knee

Apology
Take the knee

You, me
Take the knee

Everybody
Take the knee

The President and The Bible
#81 / 04:06:2020

Blasphemous, irreverent
The photo of the President

The Bible is not resident
In the White House of the President

Jesus is not evident
In the actions of the President

Godliness – irrelevant
In the outlook of the President

Ignorance that's eloquent
In the backlash of the President

Only stone and sediment
In the hard heart of the President

No room needs this elephant
The presence of this President

Darkness that's malevolent
Prevalent in this President

Hell Raiser

for Steve Priest
#82 / 05:06:2020

Top of the Pops
Was always worth watching because of you
If only to see what our dads would say

We hadn't got a clue – what to do!
But we still said it like you
In the schoolyard on a Friday

Dodgy make up
Hot pants and Red Indian head-dresses
German helmets and silver platform boots

And always a knowing smile
A wink to the camera
A pout, a kiss and a flounce

We didn't know what "camp" was then
We just knew it was fun
Especially with you

Not moody, mysterious or mystical
But underrated because you smiled
You rocked and rolled and entertained

And that's why we remember
That's why we loved you
We were ready Steve

Too Much to Ask?

#83 / 05:06:2020

The death toll ever rising
You failing in your task
Isn't it a little late
To suggest that we all wear a mask?

Surely the time for action
Was way back in the past?
So why now? Why and how?
Should we now wear a mask?

You gambled with our lives
The die – it has been cast
And now and only now you say
That we all should wear a mask?

You didn't close the airports
The lockdown didn't last
Suddenly – it's common sense
That everyone should wear a mask?

Guidelines that aren't followed
Back to normal far too fast
A practical solution
Ooh – let's all wear a mask

Is the question difficult?
Is it too much to ask
Why? Oh why? Oh why? Oh why
Is now the time to wear a mask?

Phone Call From a Friend
#84 / 06:06:2020

Finally, we talked
Missed calls, months passed
A few texts here and there
But finally we talked … and talked

Of families and illness
The state of the world
How our lives have changed
And the ways we now fill our time

Not gigs on the road and tours
But ways to roast a chicken
Or baste a pork joint
Spice racks and whether we've ever used cumin

We were never rock and roll
But we miss the audience connection
The interaction of voices
And the communion of something special

Remembering Steve Priest and the like
Childhood days revisited
Waiting for our dad's predictability
With those glam rock ugly sisters

Time passed easily, time passed quickly
Eulogising over the genius of "How Does it Feel"
"Tiger Feet" and how bands that had a laugh
Were never given the credit they deserved

Mutual musical recommendations
Common ground excavated
It was great not to be isolated
To make contact, to laugh, really laugh

We said that maybe we'd write a song
My words – your music and voice
But if we don't, no worries
It was just great to hear your voice

Next time we'll talk for even longer
Face to face
With good quality beer
Cheers John, cheers

Malady in the U.K.

#85 / 07:06:2020

In the first days of lockdown
When streets were empty
Town centres ghostly
Strangely, there was hope

People helped each other
Took it all seriously
Clapped the N.H.S. from doorsteps
Isolation meant isolation

It felt like there was hope
A chance to change
A time to somehow start again
Something new

All gone now
Worse than it's ever been
Clamouring for normality
In the face of mortality

Social distancing ignored
Gathering to drink and litter
Or protest, march – and worse
Mixed messages and chaos

Government – a laughing stock
Clowns – but no jokes
Deadly serious pantomime
But this is not behind us

Oh no it isn't

Weekend Haiku Thoughts
#86 / 08:06:2020

If statues must fall
From when black lives were worthless
Tear these relics down

Black lives must matter
And white lives must understand
Now more than ever

No grey areas
What is right is right is right
These lives must matter

Are We Being Served?
#87 / 09:06:2020

Like an out of date sitcom
All catchphrases and stereotypes
Predictable plots and quotable lines
But are we being served?

The joke seems to be on us
As the Prime Minister makes a cameo
Like young Mister Grace as the credits roll
Saying "You're all doing very well!"

Meanwhile …
We have all been watching

Empathy Day or ... Irony Day?

#88 / 10:06:2020

On Empathy Day
You spoke of tolerance and
How black lives matter

The same empathy
When talking "picaninnies"
"Watermelon smiles"?

Lesson – the Danger ... or is it Lessen the Danger?

#89 / 10:06:2020

Stop – start – school – all of this mess meant
Ineffective risk assessment
Differing views – changing lately
Inconclusive health and safety

I'm Forever Bursting ...

#90 / 11:06:2020

We've got a new term
To help us all learn
But the problem and the trouble is
We don't have a clue
Just what we should do
We don't know what a bubble is

Sometimes

#91 / 12:06:2020

Sometimes it's affirmation
Sometimes collaboration
Sometimes we need creation
Just to get through

Sometimes it's family
A friend reaching out to me
Sometimes it's poetry
Just to get through

Sometimes it's resistance
To anti-social distance
Asking for your assistance
Just to get through

Lose myself with Stephen King
Listening to Michael sing
Sometimes the little things
Just to get through

Sometimes it's not enough
To be loved by the ones you love
Sometimes it's other stuff
Just to get through

Sometimes you've got to say
Today's a day that's not okay
Tomorrow is another day
Just to get through

The Singer Sings His Song – with a Poet's Heart

for Michael McDermott
#92 / 13:06:2020

Every word is sacred
Not a word is wasted
Heavy with their truth, they hit every single mark

Every word is vital
Every line and every title
The singer sings his song – with a poet's heart

Every word is real
Nothing is concealed
Honesty that's harrowing, each heart string torn apart

Every word is open
Every word is broken
The singer sings his song – with a poet's heart

Every word has meaning
A reason for believing
Precious like the diamonds, shining in the dark

Depth and understanding
Important and demanding
The singer sings his song – with a poet's heart

Every word is whole
Directly from the soul
Reaching out to touch us - with a healing spark

Every word connects us
A hit to the solar plexus
The singer sings his song – with a poet's heart

The power of the story
The pain and then, the glory
The singer sings his song – with a poet's heart

Every word is honest
Reflecting what's upon us
The poet writes his poems with a singer's art

Welcome Back
#93 / 13:06:2020

COVID times, Twitter frozen
We miss all the words you've chosen
Poet, friend – to those who knows him
Michael – risen, Michael Rosen

Truth

#94 / 14:06:2020

Trouble in these troubled times
Join the dots and see the signs
Try to read between the lines
Looking for the truth

Liberty for statues
Monuments as public loos
Can't believe what's in the news
Just what is the truth

Protest and resistance
Singing songs of Winston's
Shouting their insistence
Standing up for truth

Saluting like a Nazi
Polluting all our history
Diluting all the bravery
Pissing on the truth

Honouring all those deceased
All the ones who died for peace
By picking fights with police
Fighting for the truth

Black lives, white lives
Fake news and Twitter lies
Those who cry the loudest cries
Shouting for the truth

Just who is fighting who
Nobody has got a clue
What is false and what is true
Questioning the truth

Trouble in these troubled times
Join the dots and see the signs
Try to read between the lines
Looking for the truth

Saint Patrick's Day

#95 / 15:06:2020

Patrick Hutchinson

Did the right thing
Amidst the throng of wrong

An act of selflessness
When the moment was heated

An act of calmness
When all around was chaos

An act of peace
In the theatre of hate

An act of bravery
In the time of need

He wasn't heavy
He wasn't your brother

But you carried him to safety
Leant him on your shoulder

A living example
Compassion and equality

The Twelfth of June
A new Saint Patrick's Day

I'm Not Looking Forward to Football Again

#96 / 16:06:2020

I'm not looking forward to football again
Not missing the beautiful game
My team are unbeaten since I don't know when
I'm glad to be free of the strain

I'm not looking forward to football again
It's starting but won't be the same
No doubt about it, since I've been without it
I've not had the heartache and pain

My nerves are un-shredded, my pulse rate is even
Moods – they don't dip or change
No agitation, no aggravation
My passion, it seems on the wane

I'm not really bothered but no hesitation
Now football is starting again
I've not missed the depression
But here's my confession
I'll probably watch every game

In a League of His Own

#97 / 17:06:2020

No matter our team
No matter our allegiance
We support Marcus

All children matter
Nobody should go hungry
Thank you to Marcus

If we do not care
For those who have the least then
We don't care at all

It's all kicking off
Number ten to number ten
P.M. met his match

Prime mover, great finish
Already you have scored the
Goal of the season

One Marcus Rashford
Only one Marcus Rashford
We all sing your name

Problem or Solution

#98 / 18:06:2020

Protest or anarchy
Clarity or sanity
Trying to hold on to what is our humanity

Fighting inequality
Rewriting history
Statues falling in the name of liberty

Chaos and confusion
Truth is an illusion
Bigotry and hatred, power and delusion

Black lives, white lies
Don't know who to patronise
No matter how it is described it is still apartheid

No disputing
Rioting and looting
Nobody's a winner when there's tear gas and shooting

Revolution starter
Ripping up the charter
Who you going to deify and who you going to martyr

Don't know what's next
Got to find context
As long as it's not some cop's knees on a neck

Fact or fiction
Duty dereliction
Fake news, twitter views, run for re-election

It's all getting tribal
There won't be revival
With a phony president posing with a Bible

Great Britain, U.S.A.
History won't go away
No matter what you say, things are not okay K.K.

Apologies your majesty
Your birthday was a tragedy
Loyalty to royalty transforming into travesty

Aiming for Churchillian
Vile and vaudevillian
Swastikas and Sieg Heils, repulsive and reptilian

Twitter chatter
All lives matter
True that they do but try it when they're blacker

Everybody says this
I am not a racist
Heads full of ignorance and far too scared to face this

Don't be selective
Got to get perspective
Tolerate intolerance – always ineffective

Be analytical
When everything's political
Be what you want to be but don't be hypocritical

You say you're not the problem
But this is the conclusion

You're part of the problem
At the heart of the problem
If you don't start the redemption and solution

Always the problem
Always the problem
Always the problem
Never the solution

Songbird

for Dame Vera Lynn
#99 / 19:06:2020

Your voice, synonymous with war
Your songs of love and peace
Like the girl who sang next door
Of hope and sweet release

Of sweethearts who will re-unite
Whenever that may be
Bluebirds flying, cliffs of white
If we just wait and see

The purest melody that starts
For every woman, every man
An angel voice that caught our hearts
Like everybody's favourite nan

Timeless songs live ever more
Thanks to you, Dame Vera
Fare thee well, we sing along
The ending of an era

Tired

#100 / 20:06:2020

I'm tired of writing angry poems
Tired of being frustrated
Tired of depressing headlines
To be honest, I'm just tired

Tired of watching the news
Tired of shouting at the television
Tired of the excuses and lies
Really tired

Tired of endless days the same
Tired of wearing these clothes again
Tired of isolation and silence
Just tired

Tired of not being able to work
Tired of the uncertainty
I'm not doing a great deal
But I'm still tired

If this is tired
Don't want to be retired

All the World is a Plague – a Sonnet
#101 / 20:06:2020

This lexicon of emptiness rings out
This condescending clanging of a bell
Cliched platitudes leave us in no doubt
Your hands-on handles on the cart to hell

Unprecedented times though these may be
These levels of ineptitude just rise
Everyone is shouting – at you on the T.V.
As questions go unanswered with the lies

This bumbling trickery with smiling face
The frippery of painting of a plane
A shameful farce the waste of track and trace
A footballer who doesn't have a name

Shakespearean is something he would be
A comedy of errors – that is he

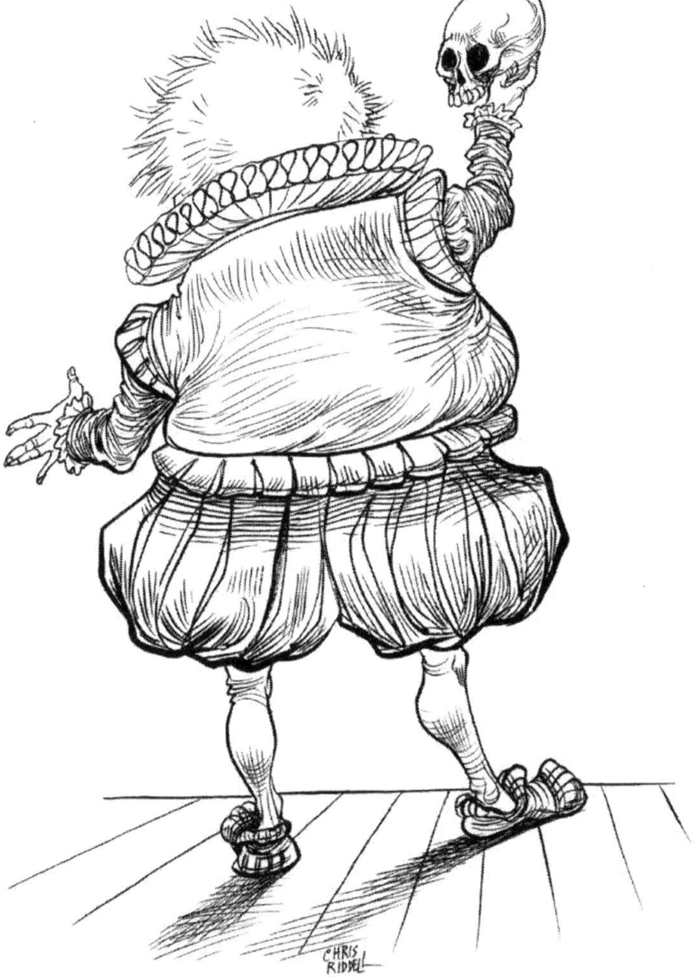
CHRIS
RIDDELL

Boris – On It? Boris – Sonnet
#102 / 21:06:2020

Well – erm – ha – harrumph – er – well – ha – you see
Sentences – er – gaps – and – I'm – er … perplexed
Ahem – ah – waffle – piffle aimlessly
No idee-ah – which words – um – come out … … next

Absolutely! Hmmm – and – cough – and-and-and
Aha – you see – I – I – I – I – mutter
A random pause – erm – I – don't – und – errr – stand
If in doubt – st – st – st – st – stutter

Yes – yes – yes – yes – I mean it – standing here
Proud and in control – total and complete
Let me be transparent and quite clear
Repeat – repeat – repeat – repeat … repeat

Feigned sincerity – this art of bluffing
Much ado – as usual – about nothing

Today's News – in Limerick Form
#103 / 22:06:2020

While life is generally rubbish
What needs to be understood is
In trivial news
The blues didn't lose
And these poems are going to be published

Ignorance is Bliss
#104 / 23:06:2020

White lives matter says the banner on the plane
Golliwogs on Facebook – but it's just fun and games
I've got a black friend and I treat them just the same
As the saying goes, ignorance is bliss
No. Ignorance is this

You say you like reggae, hip hop and rap
And you applaud all the sports stars who are black
But still you want Great Britain back
As the saying goes, ignorance is bliss
No. Ignorance is this

It isn't being snowflake, it isn't being woke
It isn't just a laugh and it isn't just a joke
White lives matter – sorry that I spoke
As the saying goes, ignorance is bliss
No. Ignorance is this

Open up your eyes, everything's subliminal
Do what you can – even if it's minimal
You say that you won't take the knee for a criminal
As the saying goes, ignorance is bliss
No. Ignorance is this

Don't get diverted, distracted or annoyed
By what you think you know about George Floyd
Jumping to conclusions is something to avoid
As the saying goes, ignorance is bliss
No. Ignorance is this

Look at the cause and not the catalyst
Look at the reasons why this movement must exist
Otherwise, every single point is missed
As the saying goes, ignorance is bliss
No. Ignorance is this

The twistery of history, the right and the wrong
More than just a statue and more than just a song
Ask every question if we are to move along
As the saying goes, ignorance is bliss
No. Ignorance is this

Equality's a quality that's only ever real
Where everybody starts on a level playing field
That didn't happen, that's why everyone should kneel
As the saying goes, ignorance is bliss
Don't let ignorance be this

No More Daily Briefings

#105 / 24:06:2020

No more Daily Briefings
No more looking for Boris
Just in case he appears
Where he mumbles and errs
Before passing over to the suits either side
The taking a long time
To tell us absolutely nothing
Apart from contradictory platitudes

No more Daily Briefings
No more daily wastes of time
No more games of "Who is that?"
Where ministers we've never heard of
Stand behind sloganned podiums
Armed with only clichés and half-truths
As they try and tell us that
The U.K. is doing very well.
Indeed

Not the best T.V. on screen
Not one of those "must-see-things"
Nothing that we're going to miss
No more Daily Briefings

Back to Life – Back to Reality?

#106 / 25:06:2020

Back to the pubs, the salons, the shops
As long as you stay a metre away
Have they really chosen the fourth of July
So it sounds like Independence Day?

Just what has happened to Track and Trace?
No vaccinations for those that are ill
Last time we looked at the figures
People were dying still … still

If Lockdown is easing are we on the mend?
Has COVID-19 just gone away?
Or are we just bored, impatient and stupid
To think we are safe and we'll be okay?

Churchill Would Be Proud

#107 / 26:06:2020

Blame it on the sunshine
The weather and humidity
Unprecedented times
Equalled with stupidity
Lockdown breakout causes
Police and peace-less breaches
Churchill would be proud
There was fighting on the beaches

Drink and drugs and barbecues
It's a Bournemouth D-Day
Anti-social distancing
Where the beach becomes a bidet
Invasion of the stupid
The lemmings, louts and leeches
Churchill would be proud
There was fighting on the beaches

A sad, sad day for common sense
Mob culture and mob rules
A buzzing swarm of selfishness
The gathering of the fools
The second spike that we should fight
Now looms within our reaches
Churchill would be proud
There was fighting on the beaches

Freedom is a basic right
Well worth fighting for
We're all in this together
But this is not the war

So learn from recent history
The harsh truth that it teaches
This virus is alive and viral
It will multiply and spiral
The second wave could well be tidal
And we're fighting on the beaches?

Hindsight
#108 / 27:06:2020

Hindsight, blindsight
Wrap it up how you like
Waiting for the next wave
Waiting for the second spike

Doctors that are tireless
Nurses that inspire us
All these scientists
And still we've got the virus

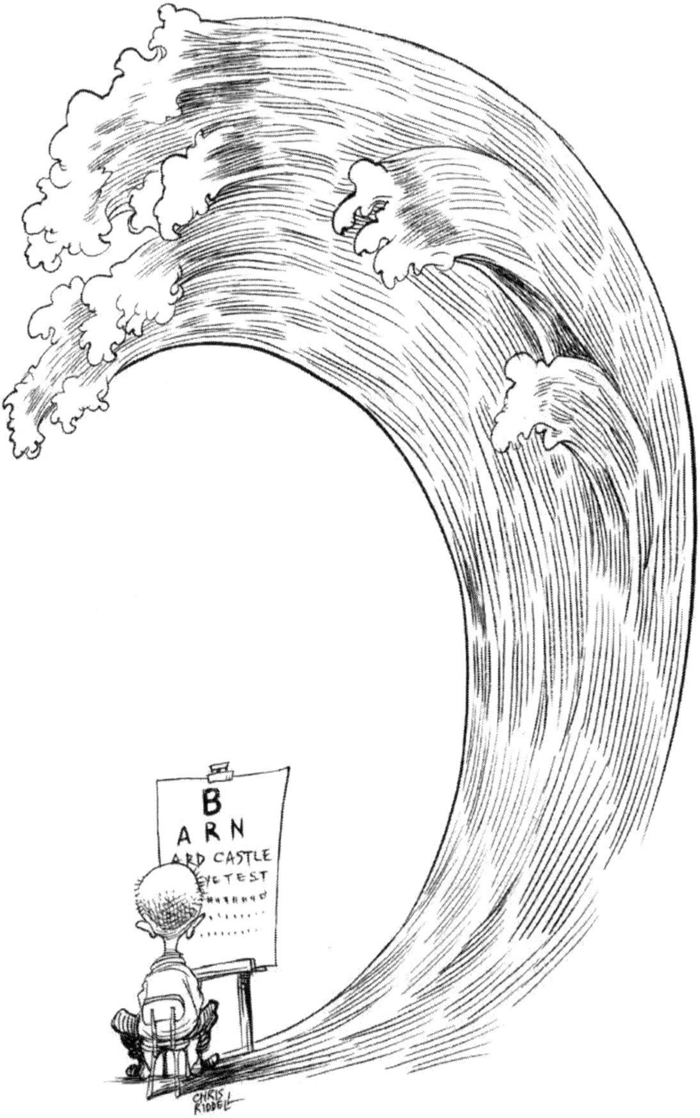
B
A R N
ARD CASTLE
YE TEST
CHRIS RIDDELL

He Wants His Churchill Moment

#109 / 28:06:2020

He wants his Churchill moment
You can tell it from his speeches
"We'll wrestle this mugger to the ground"
Fight it on the bleaches

He wants his Churchill moment
So when all this is over
It's spitfires, waffle and we'll meet
By white cliffs at Dover

He wants his Churchill moment
All fuss and bluff and bluster
And all the British bulldog
Spirit he can muster

He wants his Churchill moment
This leader who'll inspire us
Just because his legacy
Is he survived the virus

He wants his Churchill moment
Assurance and endurance
But he's more like the Churchill
That dog that sells insurance

He wants his Churchill moment
Tactician, soldier, hunter
But half of him is Flashman
Crossed with Billy Bunter

He wants his Churchill moment
A soundbite and smokescreen
We'll double down to level up
Whatever that may mean

Too little too late – too much too soon
Every ummm and every aaah
He wants his Churchill moment
Not even close – and no cigar

Fit as a Butcher's Dog
#110 / 29:06:2020

Press ups for the press
Even in my Sunday best
A shirt and tie and – yes
You've got to be impressed
Every day I exercise
Every day I jog
Bouncing back, on the attack
I'm fit as a butcher's dog

Fit as a butcher's dog you say
While smiling all agog
Fat on all the prime cuts
Now that's more like a butcher's dog

Detectives most perceptive
In this national time of need
Detectives are detecting
An increase in my speed
Back in Number Ten again
Like falling off a log
Full of beans, I'm lean and keen
Fit as a butcher's dog

Fit as a butcher's dog you say
Well – a bulldog's what you ain't
More Old English Sheepdog
Selling whitewash and gloss paint

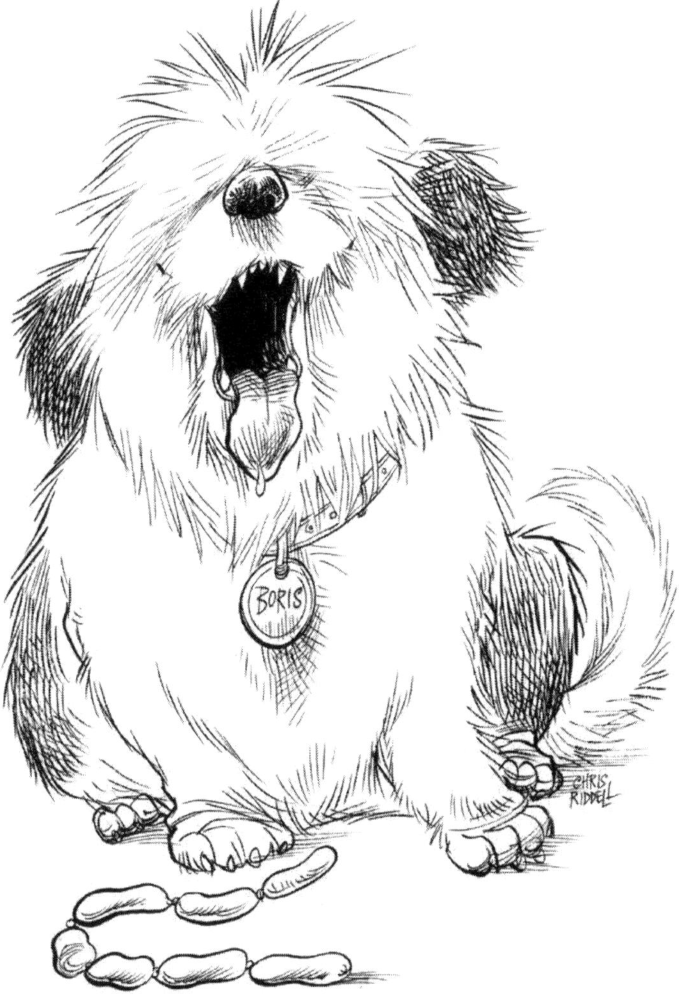
BORIS
CHRIS RIDDELL

At home I'm present and involved
In a detailed way
What all of those details are
I really cannot say
Happy to get stuck in though
Happy to do my slog
Oh yes, I changed a nappy once
Fit as a butcher's dog

Fit as a butcher's dog you say
Fit as a butcher's dog
A hound we've found that likes to sound off
Going the whole hog

Fit as a butcher's dog you say
Happy and eager to please
Like puppy that's excited
At its owner's knees

Fit as a butcher's dog you say
Getting treats for tricks
Lots of porky pies
Fetching back your master's sticks

Fit as a butcher's dog you say
Your pedigree chum keeps humming
Chop-chop – this butcher's shop
All its staff and all its stock
All the lot that you have got
Owned by a Mr Cummings

So Many Reasons, Mister Rosen
#111 / 30:06:2020

Michael
You are back
We did not know about that fifty-fifty chance
But we are so glad that you woke up
And that the coma was a comma, not a full stop

Michael
So pleased you're back with us
Much more than just much loved
More than very much missed
A national living treasure

Michael
We know your words so well
Everybody's favourite uncle
With our favourite stories and jokes
The one who pulls the funny faces
Especially when you shouldn't

Michael
You may feel feeble and lopsided
Like your legs are cardboard tubes full of porridge
But you've gone from horizontal to hobbling

Sticky McStickstick
A stick for walking is better than not walking at all
Plus it's something to wave at the telly
When your beloved Arsenal frustrate you
As indeed they will

Michael
We look forward to hearing your voice again
Reading new poems
Re-reading old poems
Retweeting all those tweets

But Michael
Sorry – we must be patient, as you have been
Leave you alone to relax, recover, gain strength
And not be distracted by our well-wishes, however kind
Or poems like this

Michael
We are glad that you are back

Michael – the voice of reason
Michael – the voice of Rosen

Boz the Builder

#112 / 01:07:2020

Boz the builder – can he fix it?
Boz the builder – yes he can!

Hard hat – hi-viz – forklift driver
Photo-op – well fulfilled
He has a got a message for us
We are going to build – build – build

Three words that he can remember
One word, three times – he is thrilled
He repeats it – and repeats it
And repeats it – build – build – build

Boz the builder – can he fix it?
Boz the builder – thinks he can

We can battle any crisis
Many workers – highly skilled
Diggers, tractors – they'll distract us
When they start to build – build – build

Let's all clap the wealth creators
Bankers, merchants – of the guild
Working together to get the job done
You will all be billed – billed – billed

Boz the builder – can he fix it?
Project Speed – spend – spend – spend
Bodge the builder – here's to Brexit
We will all pay in the end

Let Me Tell You How I Count the Days
#113 / 02:07:2020

I count the days in custard creams
Today – seventeen

I mark the hours with cups of tea
A personal record – twenty-three

Every quarter of an hour I need
To see my latest twitter feed

Another twenty – such an age
Count the likes on my Facebook page

Wander round the house a bit
Pick a book up, look at it

Kettle on – another cup
Catch up on the washing up

Telly on – flick around
Sit down – get up – sit back down

Messenger and email checks
Solitaire – read a text

Click the mouse – surf the net
Who my team is playing next

Toilet time – magazine
Articles already seen

Notebook open – pick up pen
Three lines later – down again

YouTube lotto, Instagram
It may be vague – but it's a plan

Let me count up all the ways
To fill the time on lockdown days

Can't Wait for Saturday Night
#114 / 03:07:2020

I'd love to go down the pub again
Too long a wait for a night with friends

I've missed the crack, the atmosphere
Football chatter, hand-pulled beer

Things may start with good intentions
Two pints later – not a mention

No such thing as social distance
Another pint – no resistance

Have another mate – it'll be right
You won't catch COVID here tonight

Fuzzy haze – defences drop
No control – too late to stop

The blurred, the slurred, the slow to think
Potential danger with every drink

I'd love to go down to the pub again
But when it's safe – I'll go there then

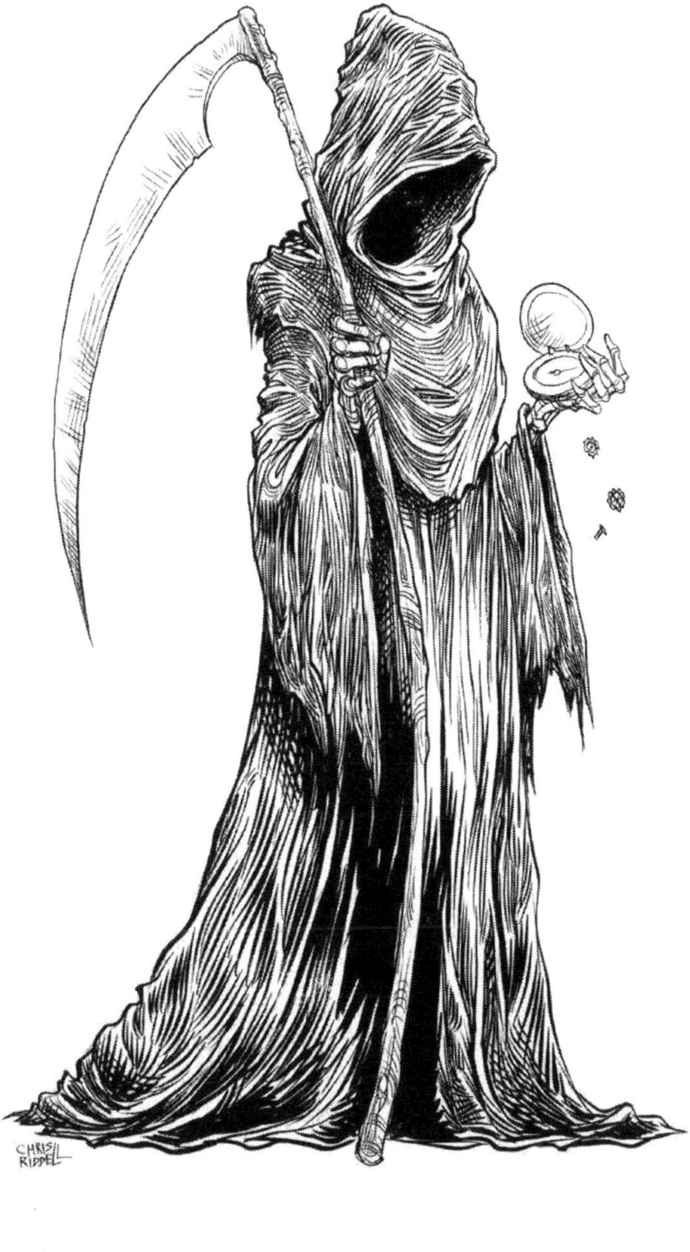
CHRIS RIDDELL

Paul Cookson
Can of Worms
Covid 19 Poetry Diary

VOL 2

Spring 2021